AF470684

First published in Great Britain by Zero To Ten Limited,
part of the Evans Publishing Group,
2A Portman Mansions, Chiltern Street, London W1U 6NR
© 2005 Zero To Ten Limited
Text © 2005 Meg Clibbon
Illustrations © 2005 Lucy Clibbon

British Library Cataloguing in Publication Data
Clibbon, Meg
Lots of love
1. Love – Juvenile literature
I. Title
152.4'1

ISBN 1 84089 376 1

Printed in China

Lots of Love X

from Meg and Lucy

with love
to Jaki and Johnny

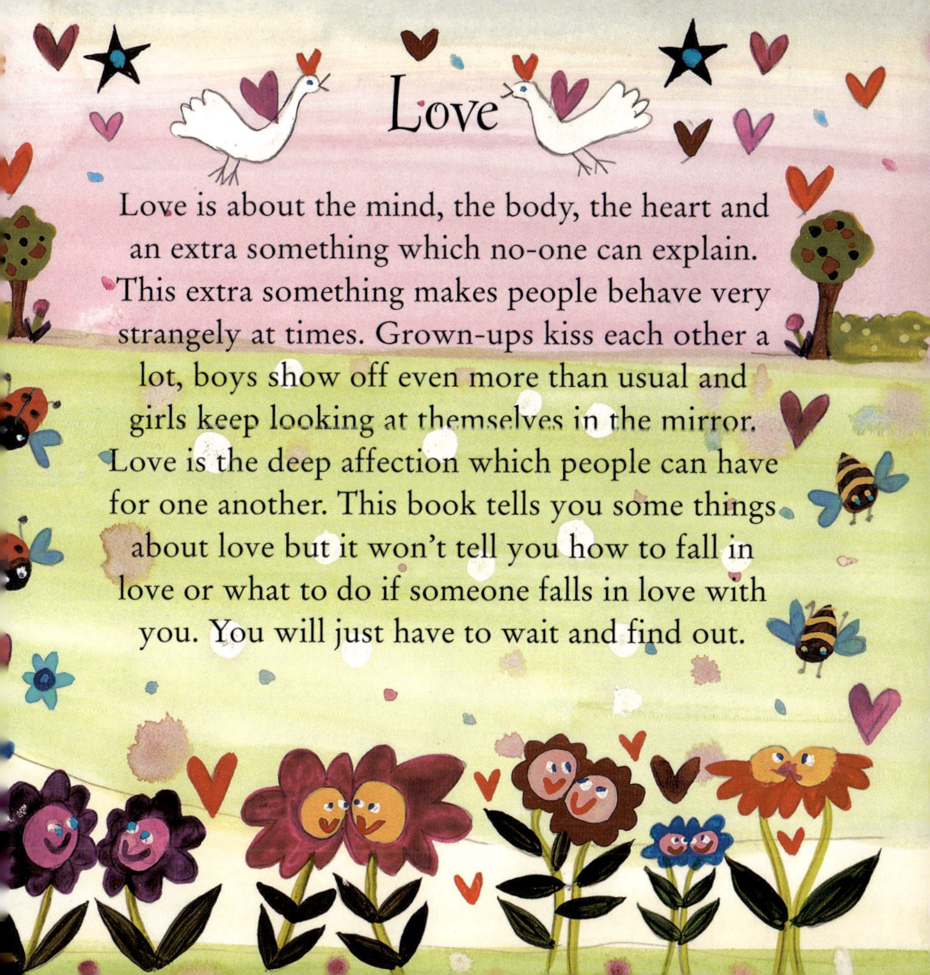

Love

Love is about the mind, the body, the heart and an extra something which no-one can explain. This extra something makes people behave very strangely at times. Grown-ups kiss each other a lot, boys show off even more than usual and girls keep looking at themselves in the mirror. Love is the deep affection which people can have for one another. This book tells you some things about love but it won't tell you how to fall in love or what to do if someone falls in love with you. You will just have to wait and find out.

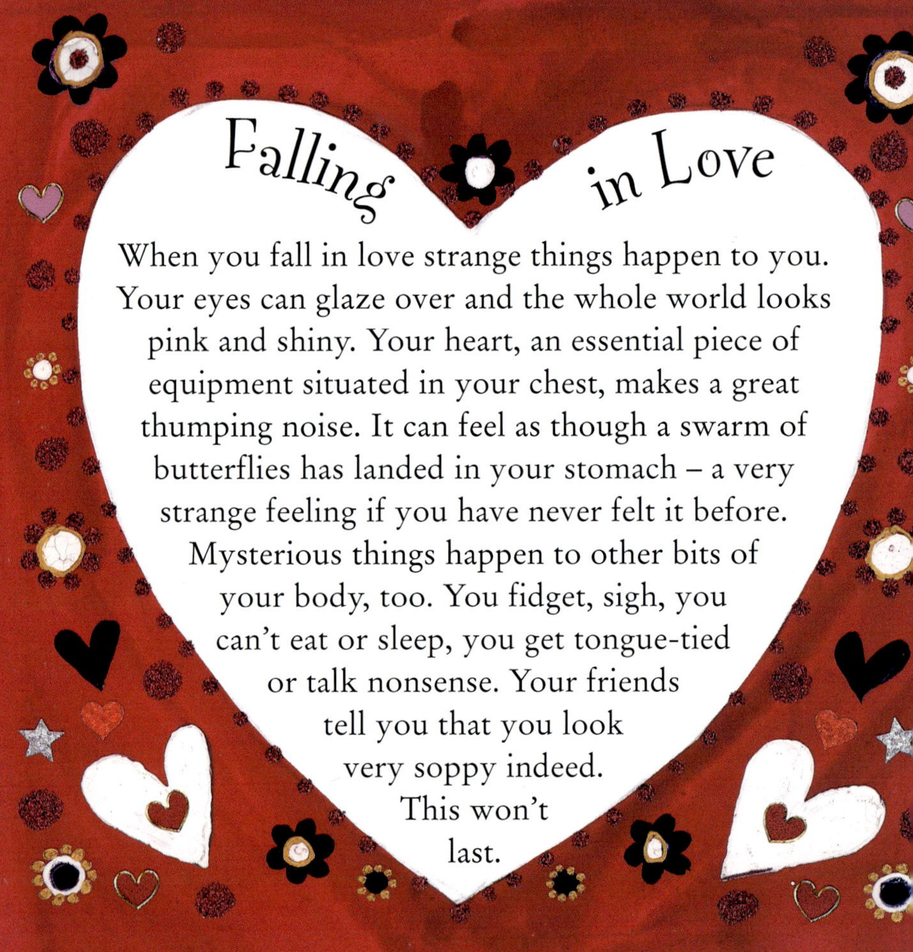

Falling   in Love

When you fall in love strange things happen to you.
Your eyes can glaze over and the whole world looks
pink and shiny. Your heart, an essential piece of
equipment situated in your chest, makes a great
thumping noise. It can feel as though a swarm of
butterflies has landed in your stomach – a very
strange feeling if you have never felt it before.
Mysterious things happen to other bits of
your body, too. You fidget, sigh, you
can't eat or sleep, you get tongue-tied
or talk nonsense. Your friends
tell you that you look
very soppy indeed.
This won't
last.

Love Victims

St Valentine

Long ago, a Roman centurion fell madly in love with a young Christian girl but they weren't allowed to marry each other. However, a holy bishop heard of their love and helped them – eventually he conducted the marriage ceremony in secret. After this many young people went to see the bishop, whose name was Valentine, and he gave them flowers from his garden and blessed them, which strengthened their love. When he died he had helped so many people that he was made a saint.

On 14th February people celebrate
St Valentine's Day by giving each other
flowers, going to restaurants, and
sending anonymous cards.

The Love Gods

These are gods and other figures from Ancient Greek
and Roman mythology still remembered today.

Venus

The Roman goddess of love who
was amazingly beautiful – she brought
joy to Gods and humans.
The Greeks called her Aphrodite.

Adonis

The Roman god of love was strong
and handsome. The Greeks called him Eros.

Cupid

A dear little god-let with a bare bottom who
flew around with a bow and arrow. Each
arrow was a love dart and if you got shot
with one of these you fell madly in love.

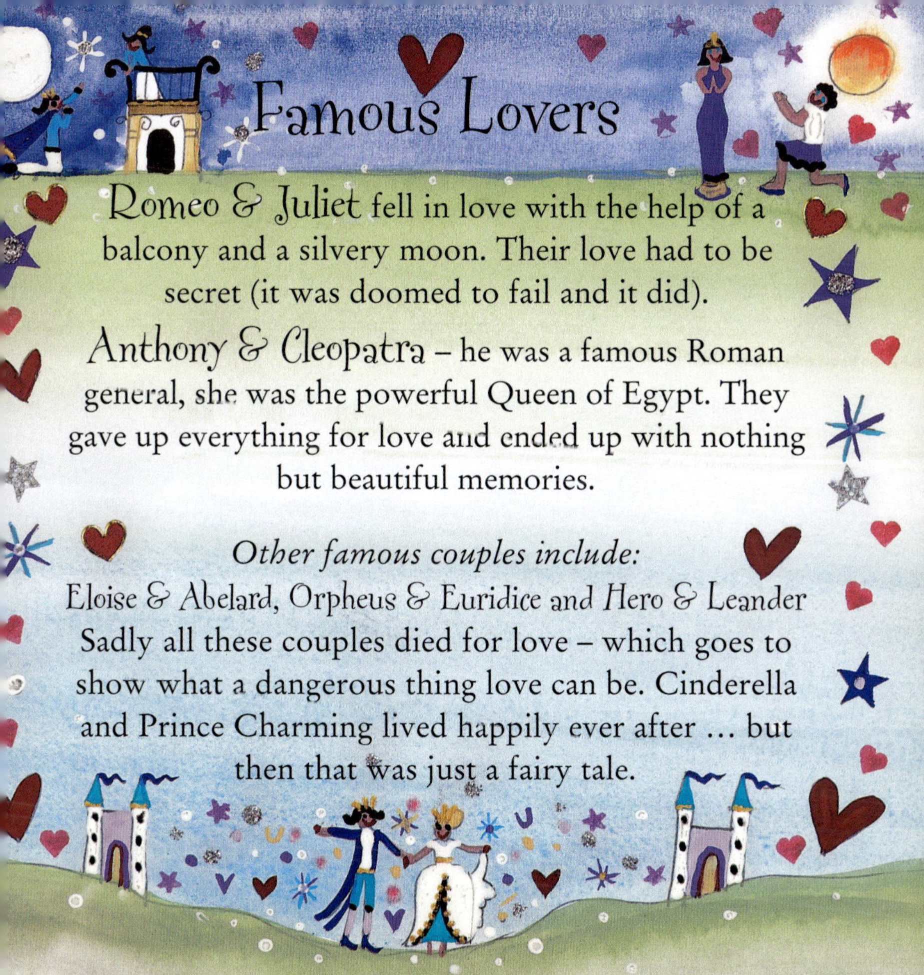

Famous Lovers

Romeo & Juliet fell in love with the help of a balcony and a silvery moon. Their love had to be secret (it was doomed to fail and it did).

Anthony & Cleopatra – he was a famous Roman general, she was the powerful Queen of Egypt. They gave up everything for love and ended up with nothing but beautiful memories.

Other famous couples include:
Eloise & Abelard, Orpheus & Euridice and Hero & Leander Sadly all these couples died for love – which goes to show what a dangerous thing love can be. Cinderella and Prince Charming lived happily ever after … but then that was just a fairy tale.

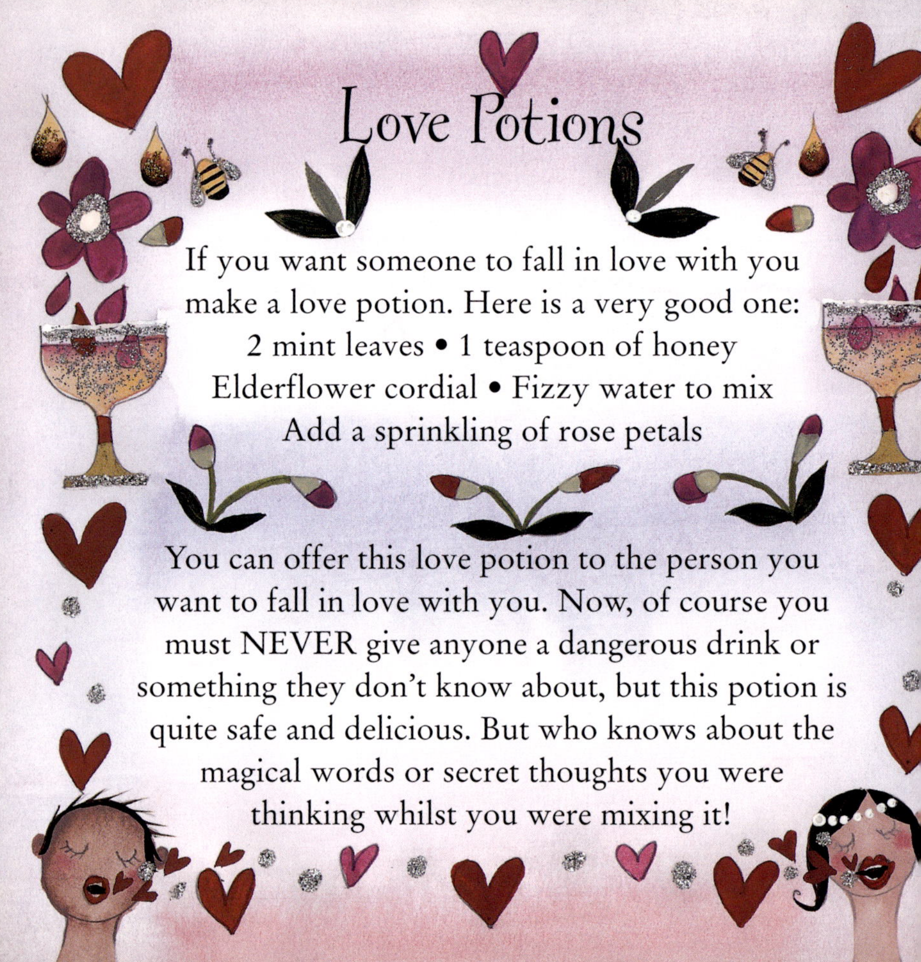

Love Potions

If you want someone to fall in love with you make a love potion. Here is a very good one:
2 mint leaves • 1 teaspoon of honey
Elderflower cordial • Fizzy water to mix
Add a sprinkling of rose petals

You can offer this love potion to the person you want to fall in love with you. Now, of course you must NEVER give anyone a dangerous drink or something they don't know about, but this potion is quite safe and delicious. But who knows about the magical words or secret thoughts you were thinking whilst you were mixing it!

Flirting

Flirting is a little love game which people play when they don't know someone very well or they want to know someone a bit better, or they know someone very well and just like playing harmless little love games anyway. Flirting involves plenty of smiling, fluttering eyelashes and lots of compliments. Flirting can often lead to falling in love but it rarely continues into marriage.

Kissing

Kissing is a very complicated activity and it is important to get it right. There are lots of different kinds of kisses and various methods to master. Here are some important guidelines:

- It is compulsory to kiss aunts, grandmothers and other elderly relatives. A brief kiss on the cheek will do but do try to smile while doing it.
- Grown ups are always kissing each other. They do it when they meet. They kiss the air on one side of the face and then the other side. Sometimes they do it three times but this is a bit excessive.
- Although kissing is rather unhygienic, never rub a kiss away, especially when the person who has kissed you is still looking.

A step by step guide to kissing for those in love

- ♥ Brush your teeth before starting this activity.
- ♥ It is helpful to approach the person to be kissed with a charming smile and a bunch of flowers.
- ♥ Pucker up the lips and make contact.
- ♥ Remember to breathe!
- ♥ This can be repeated at will but you may need to put the flowers down at some stage.

Did you know:

The Romans had twelve different ways of kissing.

Boys know when girls want to kiss them because they look at their mouths. This is a secret.

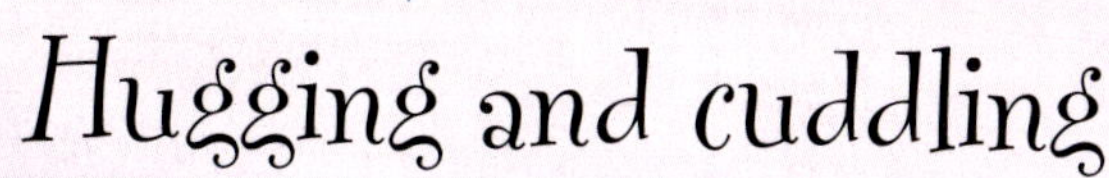

Hugging and cuddling

Hugging and cuddling are ways of expressing love for someone. A big hug makes you feel safe and special. Cuddling with the right person is like being wrapped in a warm, bubbly duvet that floats you away to a magical land. Cuddling with the wrong person is hell.

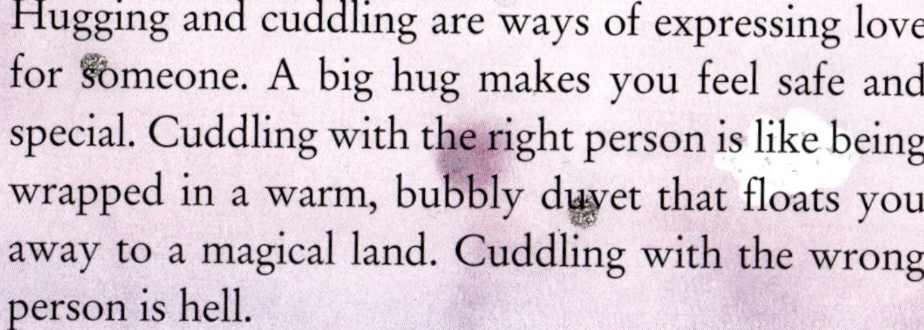

Love Sayings

'*If music be the food of love, play on*'
This could be a disaster if one likes country and western and the other likes Mozart.

'*Love means never having to say you are sorry*'
This is not true. The sooner you learn to say sorry the better. You need to say it very often even if it's very hard to do.

'Love is sweet'
This is true, but chocolate is
sweet too and a lot less trouble.

'Love will find the way'
This is not true. Many people
who claim to be in love argue about
map reading and end up in
completely the wrong place!

'All you need is love'
If only this was true! Sadly
most people need more
practical nourishment like
food and drink as well.

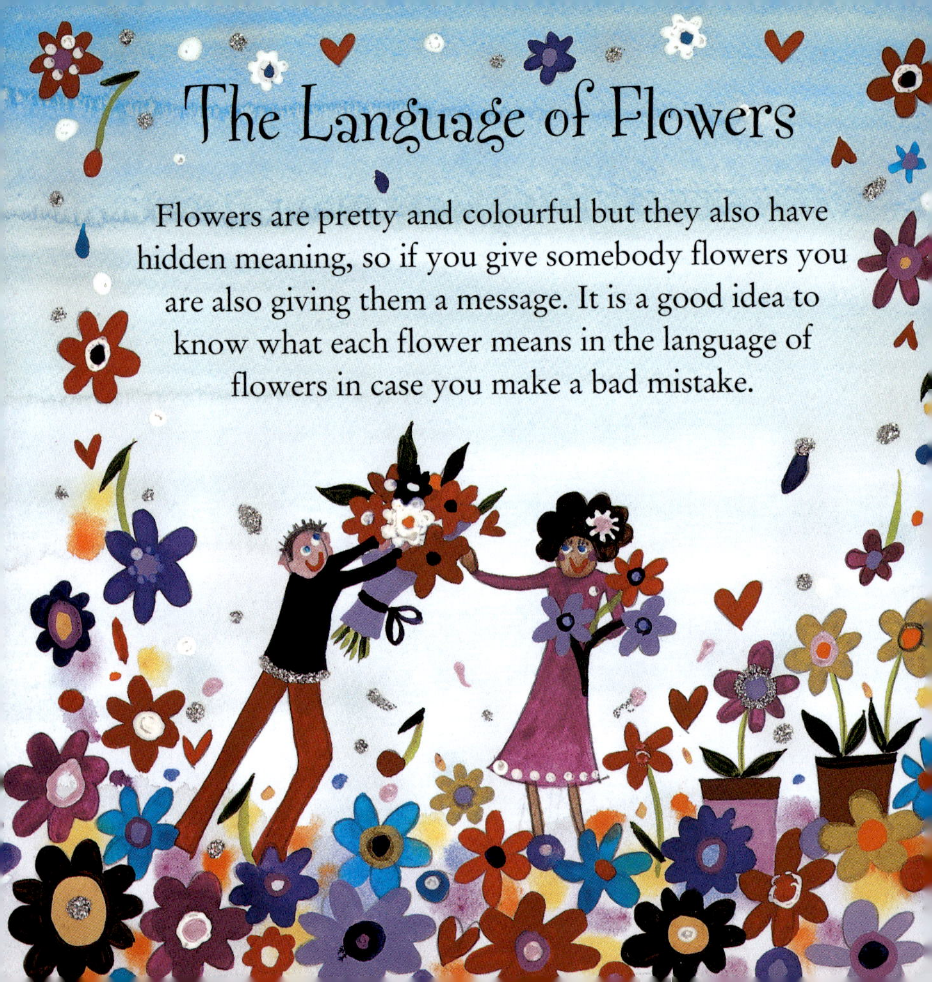

The Language of Flowers

Flowers are pretty and colourful but they also have hidden meaning, so if you give somebody flowers you are also giving them a message. It is a good idea to know what each flower means in the language of flowers in case you make a bad mistake.

<table>
<tr>
<td>

Red carnation
I am heartbroken

</td>
<td>

Chrysanthemum
I love you

</td>
<td>

Geranium
I can't wait to see you

</td>
</tr>
<tr>
<td>

Daffodil
I quite like you

</td>
<td>

Red rose
You are beautiful

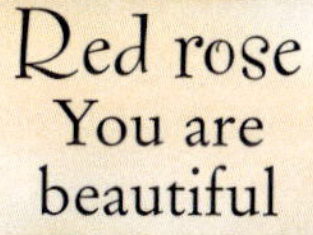

</td>
<td>

Yellow tulip
You don't stand a chance

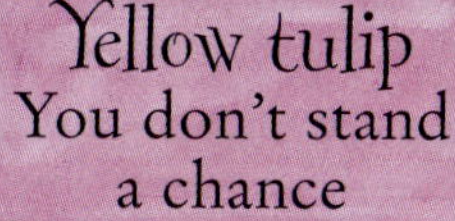

</td>
</tr>
</table>

Love birds

The swallow, the dove and the swan are love birds
but all birds are supposed to marry on February
14th, St Valentine's Day. They make their nests
and sing love songs to each other as they groom
each other's feathers and touch beaks.

The phoenix, a magical bird of myth and legend,
is a symbol of love renewed because at the
moment of death it sets itself alight and beats the
flames with its wings. Then from the ashes comes
a new bird full of new life and new love.

Love makes you want to
sing like a bird and fill
the world with music.

Rings

The most ancient symbol of love is the ring. Circles have no ending and no beginning, so a ring shows enduring love and a journey without end. Just as the earth and the moon encircle the sun so do lovers revolve around the image of perfect love – this often spirals out of control!

An 'engagement' ring is given when lovers promise to marry each other. An eternity ring is given when two people have been together for a very long time.

Gemstones

Like flowers, each gemstone is supposed to mean
a different thing:

Emerald	Ruby	Sapphire
hope and peace	passion	constancy
Opal	Amethyst	Diamond
tenderness	happiness	great love

A diamond is supposed to be a girl's best friend.
This depends on the age of the girl. A little girl prefers
hamsters and cuddly toys. However an older girl
will be happy with as many diamonds as she can get.

Love

Love is a little word with huge meanings. No single word can hold all the meanings of love. You can say that you love:

your parents    your pet    chocolate    a football team

flowers    God    dolphins    your best friend

and it would all be true. Loving your parents is like being in an old, comfy sofa you can snuggle up in or jump up and down on. Loving a football team is a kind of madness. Loving chocolate is possibly the best!

When you don't get enough to drink you are thirsty.
When you don't get enough to eat you are hungry.
When you don't get enough love something precious
deep inside you feels a bit empty. But the wonderful
and magical thing about love is that the more you give
away the more comes back to you and the people
who are full of love to give and receive are the luckiest
people in the world. Their lives are full of starlight
and sunshine, moonbeams and magic.